THIS COLORING BOOK BELONGS TO:

.................................

DATE:

.................................

Some graphic elements in this book have been created by Starline, Macrovector, Winkimages - Freepik.com

No portion of this publication may be reproduced or transmitted in any form or by any means, electronic or mechanical, including, but not limited to, audio recordings, facsimiles, photocopying, or information storage and retrieval systems without explicit written permission from the author or publisher.

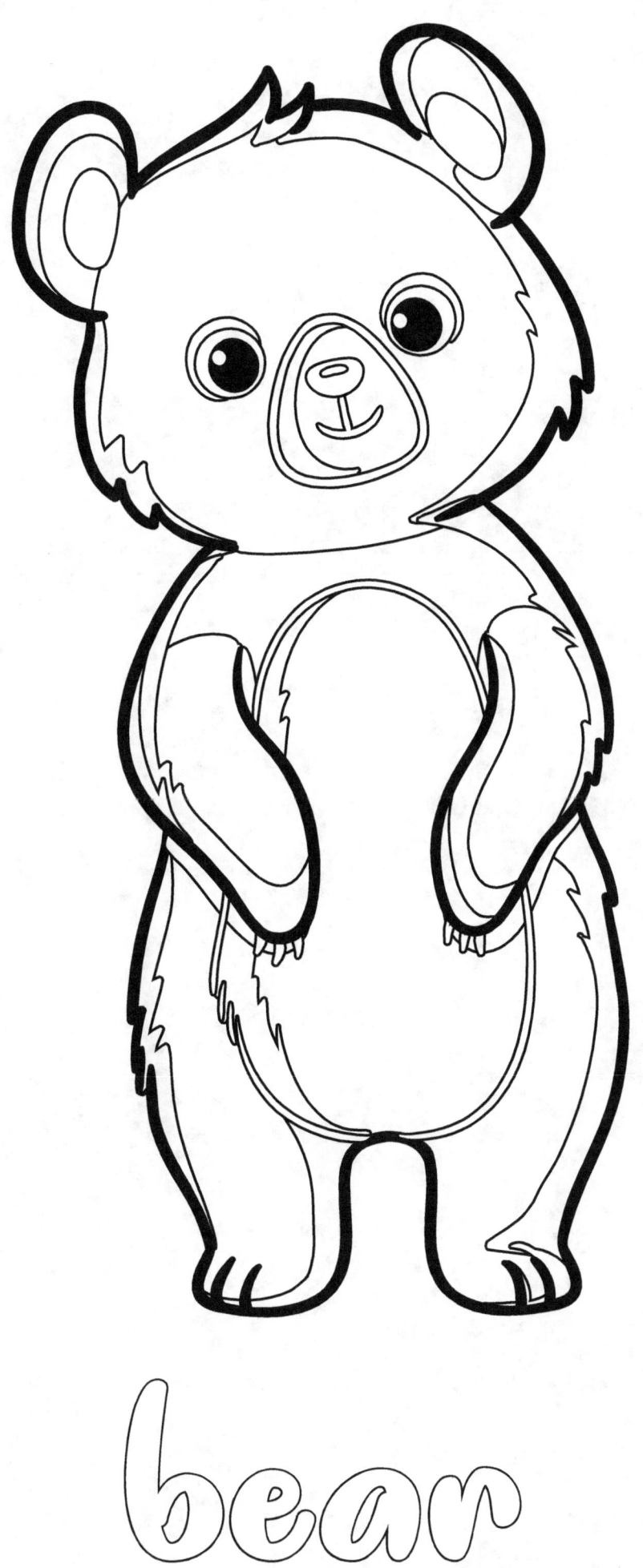

COW

flamingo

fox

goat

hedgehog

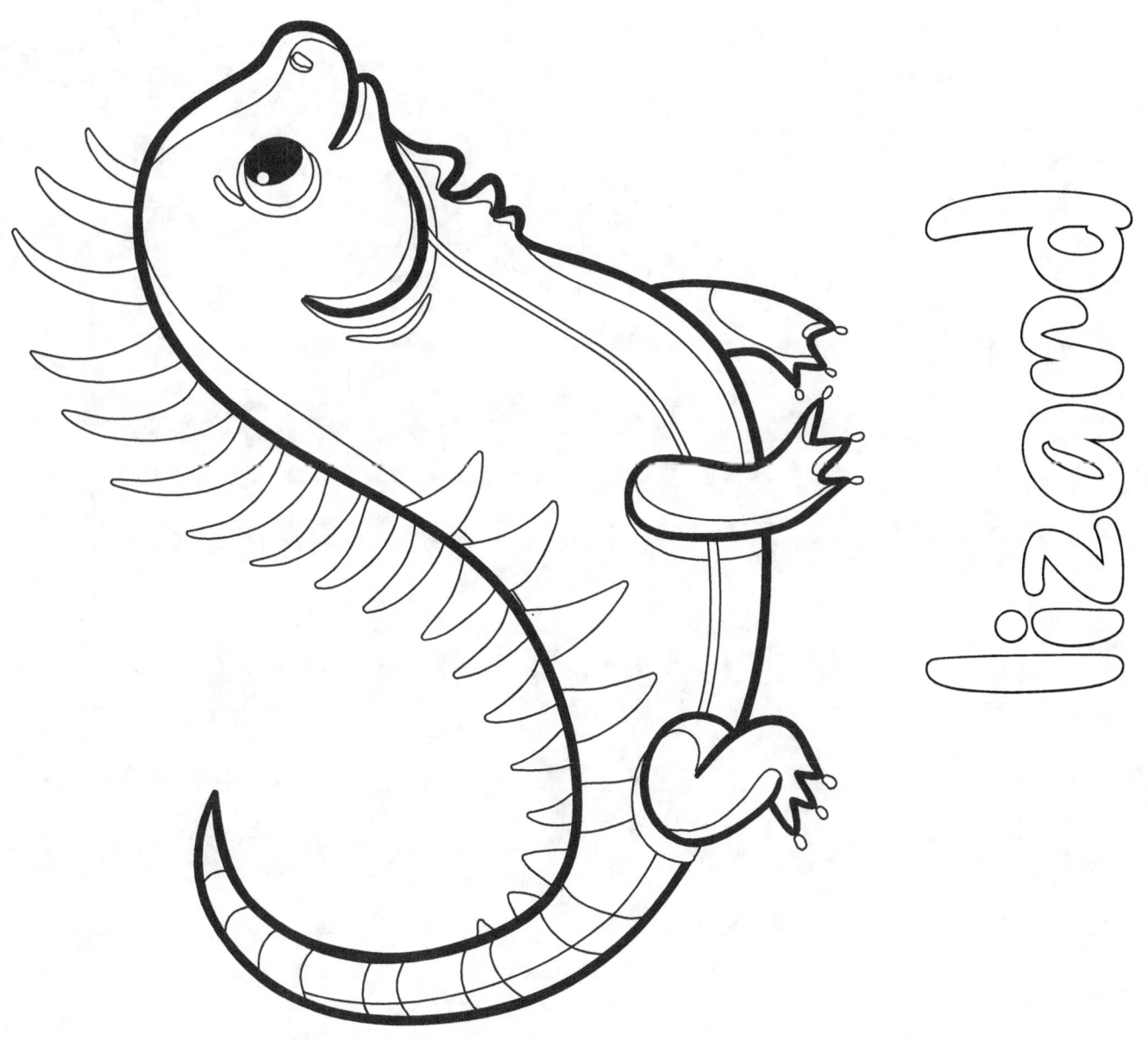

lizard

monkey

polar bear

seahorse

skunk

snake

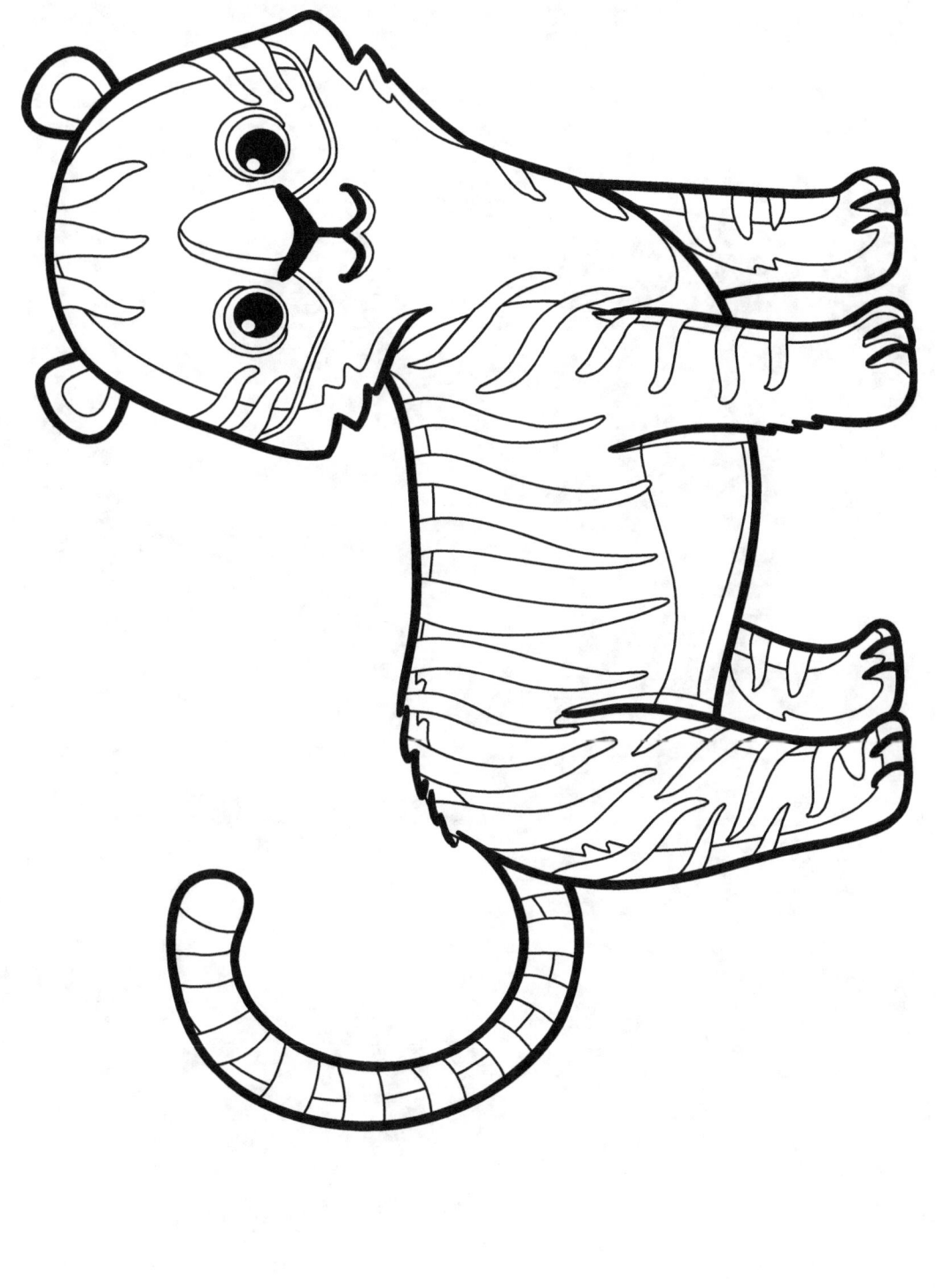

tiger

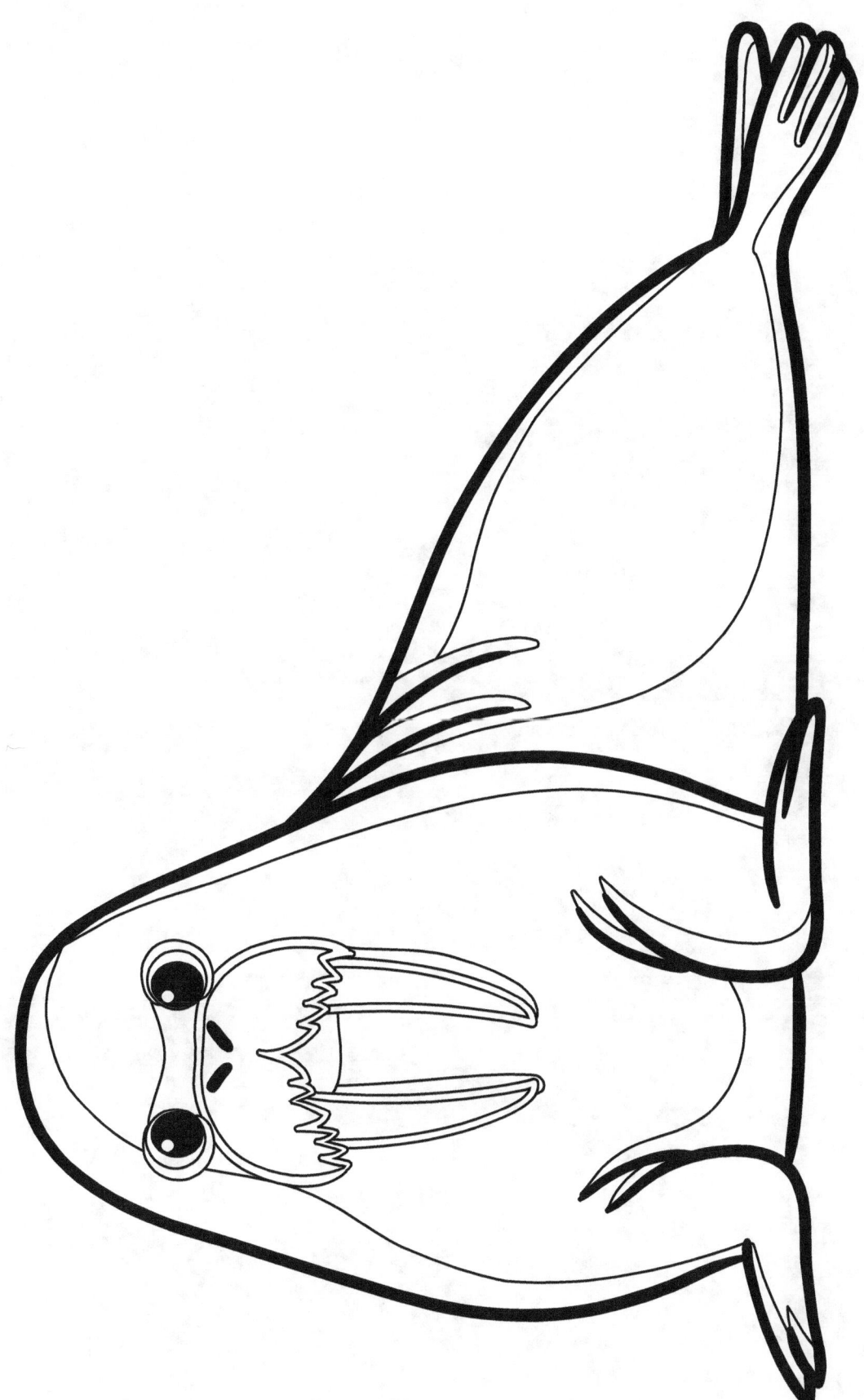

walrus

I love animals because ...

I love animals because ...

www.ingramcontent.com/pod-product-compliance
Lightning Source LLC
Chambersburg PA
CBHW080907220526
45466CB00011BA/3493